The Language of Fractions

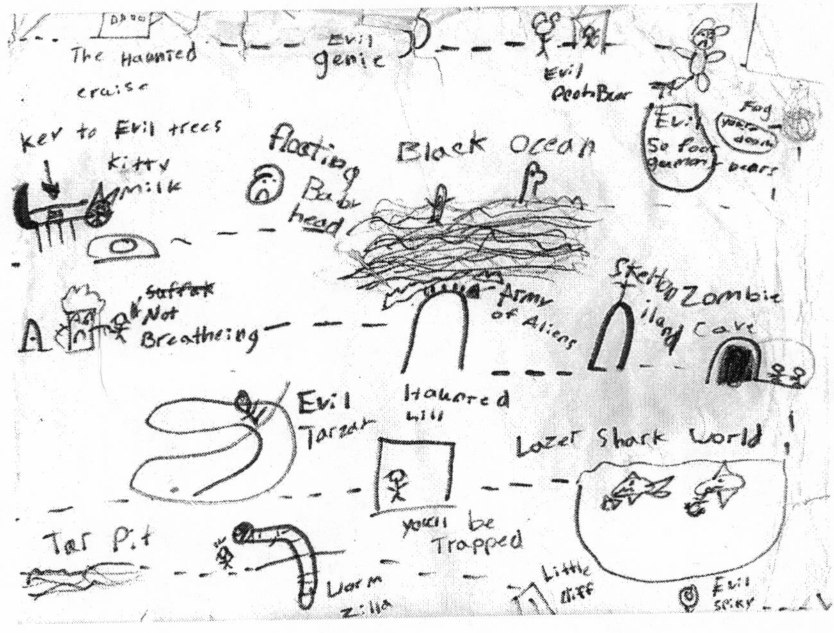

The Language of Fractions

by Nicelle Davis

~ 2023 ~

The Language of Fractions

Editor-in-chief
Eric Morago

Editor Emeritus
Michael Miller

Marketing Specialist
Ellen Webre

Proofreader
LeAnne Hunt & Victoria McCoy

Front cover art
Hues Trần

Author photo
Hues Trần

Book design
Michael Wada

Moon Tide logo design
Abraham Gomez

The Language of Fractions
is published by Moon Tide Press

Moon Tide Press
6709 Washington Ave. #9297
Whittier, CA 90608
www.moontidepress.com

FIRST EDITION

Printed in the United States of America

ISBN # 978-1957799-13-1

for the kids

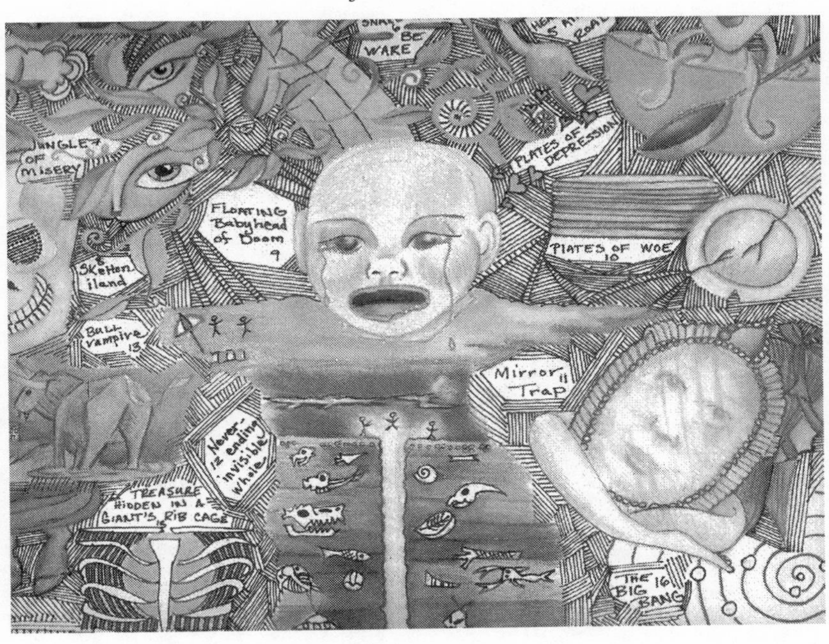

BE WARE
JUNGLE 7 OF MISERY
PLATES OF DEPRESSION
FLOATING Babyhead of Doom 9
PLATES OF WOE 10
Skelton iland
BULL vampire 13
Mirror 11 Trap
Never-ending invisible whole
TREASURE HIDDEN IN A GIANT'S RIB CAGE
THE BIG BANG 16

Contents

Foreword

Nicelle Davis' collection of poems, *The Language of Fractions,* is a collage of poems that help her readers understand the need for connectedness and living a meaningful, authentic life. Pivoting around everything from children's hand-drawn maps and her translations of them, to writing letters to different bones of the body, to the course content of a 1960's charm school syllabus, Davis playfully attempts to answer the questions around the shape of grieving, adolescence, loneliness, lining up the fractions of self in order to feel full, and developing a new center, by examining the whirlpool shaped bud we all wear, the belly button.

There is nothing more significant that represents connection but an umbilical cord. It is intentionally cut, creating a wound that forms in the center of everyone's body. It becomes a life-long reminder of both loss and of floating in fullness.

Some of the key questions Davis attempts to answer in this collection are: How many sides or variations are there to love? How do we cope with and embrace the missing parts of our lives, in fact, how can we learn to love what is missing? What does it mean to be meaningful? Will a Map Game, resembling a world built by generations before, lead the next generation through the unthinkable horrors to X marks the spot?

Some additional key themes in this collection circle around the things that keep us connected – water, blood, touch, identity, mortality and how living a meaningful life makes us more human. Davis also circles around the topic of what it means to be a woman, born or chosen. What is gender and societal expectations, when it comes? How does gender affect how humans experience love, loss and power?

When one discovers that besides his or her own personal way of living, he or she can only experience a fraction of another person's lived experience. We see everyone else only in fractions. Each person also needs to collect all the fractions of themselves and make themselves more authentically centered.

— *Annette Schiebout*

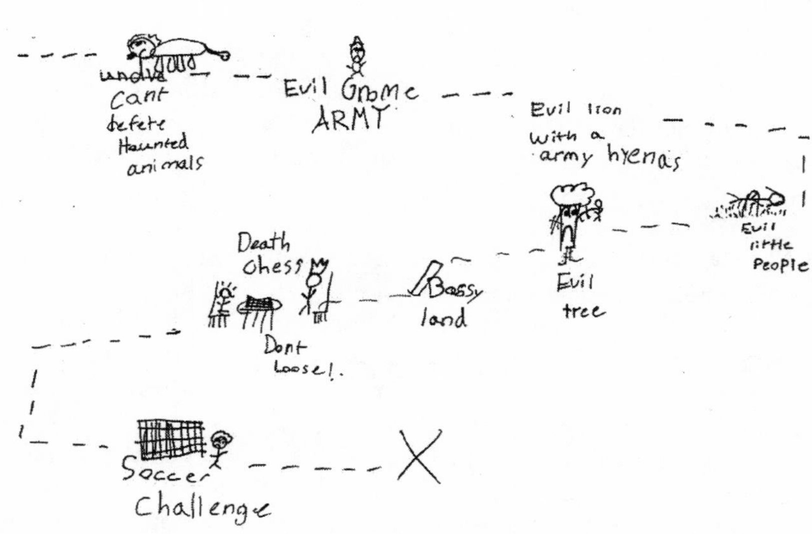

Cant
defete
Haunted
animals
Evil Gnome
ARMY
Evil lion
with a
army hyenas
Evil
little
People
Evil
tree
Bossy
land
Death
chess
Dont
Loose!.
Soccer
Challenge

0: A Love Affair

Belly Poem #1:
She Tells Me, "I Have Something You'll Like"

I.

Opening the French doors of a large wardrobe,
she takes out a severed human belly button.

The wardrobe stands like a giant *I* or *1* in the room.
What she offers from its center drawer:

discarded slice of origins, wordless poem,
door to the infinite.

Yes, I said,
I like it.

II.

…here it is as I heard it:

My friend met her years ago when living in *No-where* Arizona.
She describes her as:

a suburb-looking thing, not the type who typically appears
unannounced at desert communes.
She was after my friend's roommate, a well-known body modifier—
a scarification artist.

III.

My friend knows me well—knows all about my hours spent
documenting body augmentations— that shock of entrance
and slip from cons
    cio
        us
            ness—

I've a box of portraits showing people going some where
called pain.
It looks like an absence called pleasure.
Empty as Nirvana.

IV.

I shake the photo box for the sound of some
(one)thing rattling there. I shake this severed
skin and hear
nothing.

V.

She wanted: "her mother removed."
After days of her not leaving his front door, the Body Artist resigned to give her what she asked for—belting her to a table, he injected her with Novocain, and with a hot knife, took a palm-sized strip of flesh.

She left shortly after, telling them to burn the skin.

My friend:
couldn't bring herself to destroy it.

My friend:
kept the navel fresh in the freezer, until she had to
return to California for her mother's funeral.
My friend:
whose own mother bled to death in her arms.
My friend:
put it in a velvet box where it
shriveled to the object I was holding now

just in case: the girl wanted her mother back.

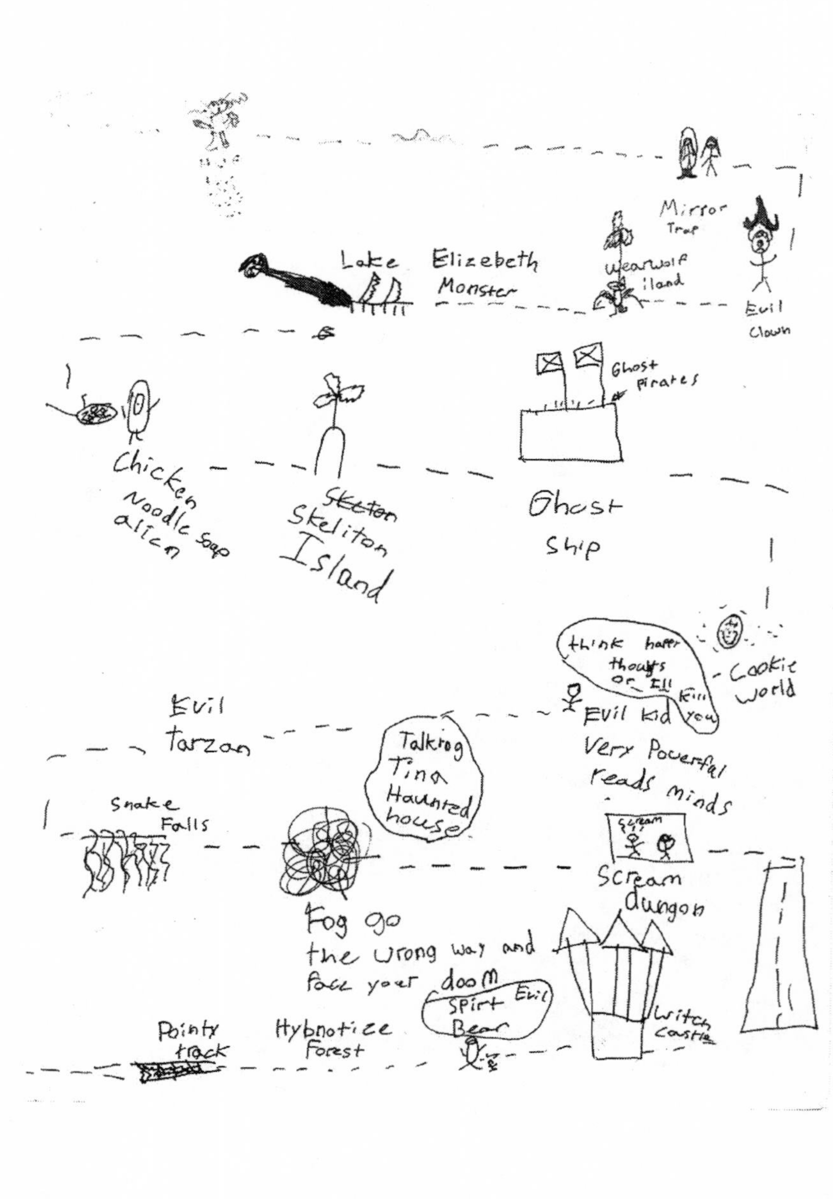

Mirror Trap
Lake Elizabeth Monster
Wearwolf iland
Evil Clown
Ghost Pirates
Chicken Noodle Soap alien
Skelton
Skeliton Island
Ghost Ship
think happy thoughts or I'll Kill you
Cookie world
Evil tarzan
Evil kid
Very Powerful reads minds
Talking Tina Haunted house
Snake Falls
scream
Scream dungon
Fog go the wrong way and face your doom
Evil Spirt Bear
Witch Castle
Pointy track
Hybnotize Forest

1/8: Love in Time

Love at Age 4: Exsanguination

It sucked me first, and now sucks thee,
And in this flea our two bloods mingled be;

—John Donne

It's not the vampires but the diseases they carry;
Lyme for example looks a lot like depression, moving
from the nervous system, to joints, to the heart.

No tick actively seeks you out. They can go two years
without eating. Reaching up toward the curved universe—
something like a hug. Entomologists call this *questing.*

So much of bug language sounds sexual. *Engorged*
to twice its size. I could see the tick in the arm of my
preschool friend—that and a row of burn marks

from where his father took a lighter to his kid's skin.
Home remedy to burn a body out of the body—
he missed and kept missing. His dad had a way of

growing dark when drinking. There are ways to love
that are larger than sexual. I held my arm to his arm,
hoping the tick would come into me.

Love at Age 5: A Question

Dishes on the floor, jewelry on a peg board, grand piano next to abandoned plastic phlebotomy practice arm. There is comfort in a lack of context, the world shuffled and randomly dealt amongst rooms. Skinned in dust, all things contained in a singular body—the auction house. I remember finding a large bowl of teeth. 25

cents a tooth then. Now it costs $200 for a dozen on Esty. I remember many molars and an endless promise for more. My belief in the Easter Bunny falling—thrill of mortality peaking. I plunged my five-year-old hand into the bowl. Watched my body dissolving inside a thousand fragmented mouths. I flipped the bowl when

a voice behind me asked, *what does it feel like*? Teeth scattered across the floor, escaping beneath China hutches and clothing racks, some landing in the toe caves of used shoes. The stranger and I fell to the ground quick as apples—trying to catch incisors before they entirely vanished. We didn't want to get caught, but caught doing *what?* Asking a question?

Love at Age 11:
This Was the Year

I was never a boy—I just didn't
want to be a girl. And you, Jehovah
Witness, didn't want to be gay.

But it was the sixth grade, and there
was a dance. The Librarian, V.P.,
and PE coach—fresh divorcees

in dated beehives and second
boob jobs, teaching us the Hustle
like our hips depended on it.

I got to teach art that year—
you taught math—
while the grown-ups smoked in

the parking lot. I guess everyone
has a list of what they don't want
to be, but are. You went against

god and filled my dance card.
I sprained your ankle. This is the year
I wore two silver and turquoise rings

on each finger. This is the year you
were whipped with a garden hose
in the shed out back. This is the year

food stopped arriving in my cupboards.
This is the year our parents fell
asleep and kept sleeping. This was

the year we fought until we bled
into one body and became, against
all odds, Brothers.

Love at Age 13:
The Middle School Scab Eater

Everything about her was recessive: hair retreating into tight curls, arms holding legs close to chest. She folded into a wooden chair like the yes / no notes we agonized over; tight origami shapes we passed while Coach wrote *heavy petting* on the board. We hated her. Her child's body and thick lips. Her shins bleeding where she ripped off scabs.

Coach going over the concept of *foreplay*, explained how the family dog never really loved us—was only after the *pleasure* of being touched. *You have to butter a lady up* was his best attempt at talking about the bodily secretions most of us were wearing like invisible gloves. She was beautiful and secretly we loved her. Her obliviousness.

In class, she blew on her open sores same as the head cheerleader blew on wet petal-pink nail polish. It was confusing, this separation of love from pleasure. She looked satisfied. Harvesting dry red chips, taking herself into her mouth like bread. She didn't notice how even Coach gagged a little when he looked at her. His argument

for abstinence, a game of averages: *If two people sleep with two people who have slept with two people,* then we've all slept with your mother and our fathers, we're all carrying something catching within us.

Love at Age 19:
Box of Ashes

The Red Iguana stayed up past the bars and was an easy stumble through the cold for hot plates of rice and beans. We walked a similar gait. A pair never meant to go together; we were always wet and exhaling smoke—understanding blood as a fire in and out of skin. These were not years with any future. Hours belonged only to the hour. The letter I wrote with my finger and flood from your broken lip, did you keep it past that night? Your tooth, I've carried across two states and twenty years. Winters thaw, and all the piss used to burn in the snow "________was here" is lost. The gold of youth guttered. Sometimes I put your punched-out molar in my mouth and call it kissing.

Love at 23:
Cuba and Coltrane

Cuba. I want to go to Cuba, where we planned to go together. Still
the smell of saving change reminds me—we didn't make it beyond
the rabid Atlantic border. You were too busy throwing boxes of
Cap'n Crunch in the yard. *Too White* for my kitchen, you said.
To match you, I threw your glossy bell peppers in the street spitting,
"I don't know how to cook this shit?" In the background the tart sound
of *A Love Supreme* played between your flesh, my flesh. Two things we
could agree on: Coltrane and Cuba. Everything else was a brood of
anger hatching. Bending to collect the scatter of yellow sugar-nuggets,
I watched you nurse a bruised pepper. Red heat in your palm. The buzz
of a horn like a nest of bees singing. Cuba. We wanted to go to Cuba.

Love at Age 25: I Wrote You a Love Letter, But You'll Think It's Gross

It's not the herpes that cause problems, they I can accept
easy as sea-monkeys—like the ad in *MAD Magazine* says,
a biological novelty turned into a reality.

I name the pink translucent marks Bob & Wanda. Always
Bob & Wanda to avoid any feelings of loss between
rejuvenations. This isn't to say

I don't notice you layer on sleepwear, incessantly wash,
beat an itch like fisting the sting out of a new tattoo, to
avoid any contact that chances me catching you. In bed

together, we think of how long it has been since the last
shock of entrance—like a ninth grader, you canoe-roll
over to my side of the mattress. We dry-

hump like summer-camp kids, quite sure / not sure, how
much better it would feel without clothes on. Nebular-wads
of toilet paper appear in the bowl. When I ask

where the floor rug has gone, you say it needs washing,
accidentally peed on, but we both know it wasn't urine that
you on(ed) the carpet with. After

weeks of not having sex the word in syllables starts to
sound as *her piece*—the Other virally stringing you along,
just as the slight hope that she may reallyreally

loveyou prompted a mid-day breakup fuck. For a week
you wrote yours & Other's name together, hoping she'd
show up like a care package full of cookies. We lie

awake together with Other between us, I think to myself
how beautiful you are overandoverandover lipping my own
tongue—imagining slimy kiss after slimy kiss.

Love at Age 32:
In the Story of Adultery that Doesn't Happen

There is a painting in the hotel lobby of trees by a river.
In the river, a reflection of something red—shape
disturbed by currents—hot color smeared across
an unwalkable pathway. This might suggest that
the sky is burning while cool tones drown the seeable
world. I keep my eyes on the painting. There is
a sense of movement in its stillness. Call it art—this
distraction from the possibility of your lips against
my saying no. Contrast of tones. I want to rub green
spring beneath your skin (dry shore) with my tongue
(damp rag)—would like to hang you on a wall (crucifix)—
pretend this is my home of five thousand rooms. Perhaps
those are not branches, but a tangle of limbs. Perhaps
those are not leaves, but silk scarves tethering hips
to the vanishing point. It's all (over)lap. Perspective.
Inside. A world. A frame. A hotel. Outside. A block
Framed by four streets. An exit unto an entrance. Repeating. Yes.
This is a mistake, I say. Logic. Red merely marks
the presence of a bird, and you are not a choice I can make—
though I would love to cup fire from this stream of brush
strokes—drink feathers—become flight—rise from the street
to be possibility. Beyond a hotel canvas—red mark.
Might be hell. But then. Might be song in midair.

Love at Age 35: Consider Exactly How Much Is Necessary in 3rd Person

Brushing sure, but not floss or mouthwash. Before you'd consider eliminating makeup, but lately you need armor when facing female co-workers. Wash the body, just pits, vaginal slit: skip shampooing hair unless there's been fire and smoke the night before. Look for a one-motion-on outfit. A dress. A coat. Sandals even in the rain. Nothing too short or tight. Make your son's lunch in time with toasted *Eggos*. Say no to bacon. Give him strawberries arranged in the shape of a heart, sugar sprinkled on top. For you Coffee. A full pot in a thermos. If only you owned two thermoses. Allow yourself a moment to think about how to write thermos in plural form. You will look half done, at least half done. This will afford you five more minutes under two comforters. One bought after you left him in your twenties—other from the absence who went back to his wife. You've given yourself too many pillows. They stack like a body—an impression of weight. With these extras, you'll have exactly three hours and thirty-five minutes in bed. Enough not to feel entirely alone by end-of-day and already undone by the day before you.

Love at Age 40: An Ordinary Love Song

Beds merger bodies; bones and blood are hard to unlearn. I needed a place to stay. This couple said they had empty space in their threesome crib. They all had their own apothecary. When she said down, he said up, and the third between couldn't digest the difference.

She died. O.D. most likely. I go years without touch—can't keep up with apathy and all its accidental orgasms. *Too sensitive*, people tell me about me. I give all my impulses to eBay. After her funeral, they went to Amsterdam for a prostitute to fill their cold spot, but the girl was

bought out from under them while they were making up their minds. What if I die a born-again virgin I (did but didn't) choose to be. My last lover told me*: all you have to do is believe it means nothing, and we can fuck forever.* I wonder, as I divide and subdivide for propagation, if

life feels alive when removed from the forest? Did I fuck up forever trying to mean something?

Love in Quarantine: Perhaps these are Not Poetic Times at All

I've become a priestess of bowel movements.
It's my daily to protect the following: carpets,
pets, and children. My neighbors have Covid.
Some more, some less. I'm always putting
my son in a poem. He and I leave the house

once a day; he smells the fair, no a farm, no
dead grass—walking he narrates each step
by scent. My dogs piss on the neighbor's cacti.
5 of 10 patients died at the across the street's
Neighbor's job. She washes linens at a retirement

home. I bleach her Christmas card before
hanging it on the tree. Her mother died today
but can't be buried until March. There's a run on
formaldehyde. She hopes to see the body
in Spring. A viewing. What's the view in March?

Or is it April? We are waiting. She loves petting
my dogs, and it takes all I have left of my human
to let her. If I died, would my dogs eat me?
I hate the idea of being taken care of. So alone
and not. What do showers bring? In the yard

where my pups shat, what's flowering? How
am I to hold the fragrance of rain with words?

Love at 42:
Dating as a Single Mom

Nothing says romance like a good horror film. The giant blue
heart painted on the white walls of the Cecil Hotel looms like
an anti-moon from your balcony. Such a vortex. Windows

looking into windows. Taste of human flesh in your tap water.
Signs all read "Pick up your dog shit" but ignore tent cities
without toilets. Where do thousands of people go when real

estate agents put on a pub crawl? Does it strike anyone else
funny that the word is REAL ESTATE—as in property makes
all things tangible. The scariest films are those where a family

gives everything for a home that wants to devour them.
The witch pulling at a child's foot that's wandered out from
under its bedsheets. I couldn't leave my bed between the hours

of midnight and 3 AM, after we watched *The Conjuring*. Dead
mothers repeating, *she made me do it.* What have we ever done
on our own accord? Such a witch makes Rosemary's rape *seem*

campy—even sweet. I guess I choose to spend every other
weekend getting scared with you—cuddled up and regressing.
We all want to be the baby sometimes.

A Love Poem is Painful, Sure but Not Torture

In death there are other deaths. The loss of one never
diminishes the other. We cry O at our start and end.
Multitudes of nothings—
zeros—holes—endless
wholes.

we are here

Map

Slow Land

Dragon castle

monster

Evil Snowman

zombie town

vampire town

Frankinstein

The most bdgest bear in the world

Cookie village

Evil monkey

Cliff

go in if you dare

spooky forest

the Haunted truck

The headlest man

knife

wach out!

T rex Land

Evil ice cream

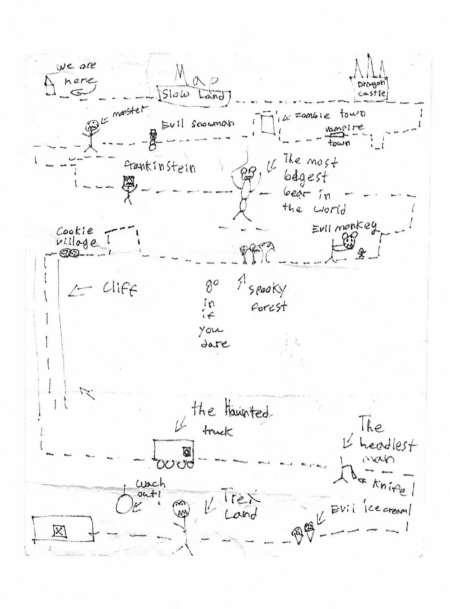

¼: Love's Gaze

Belly Poem #2: How an Affair with Part of an Unknown Woman Begins

I.

I've told this story already. Already there was / (is?)
a girl who cut her navel out. I don't know her but
I've kissed this severed piece of who?

II.

I don't know her, and I do know her. Isn't that the way
of shared flesh? Why trouble with this?—falling in with
a discarded piece of person? Tender touch. Not human
but scab. Is it wrong to touch who (or is it what) cannot
feel back? How long can I sleep with loss before giving

birth to naught?

III.

Severed human flesh held to the light of a window
glows.
The fine hairs of a woman's stomach flash as a touchable
flame.
In my hands, bright as parchment, a story I've longed to
strike.
Flesh dried to immovable permanence,
navel
twisting into itself. A wordless
language—

IV.

Every noon I birth a new us and watch it die mid-
flight. It dives beneath my feet, swimming circles
where I walk. Who have I loved well? This un-
known someone.

a wish: she'll pull me into
(wet) center—

IV.

Ladies and Gentlemen,

The *Etymology Dictionary* presents for your viewing pleasure—the Navel:

roots include *bembix*, literally "whirlpool."

Old Church: Slavonic *papuku*, originally "bud." Considered

a feminine sexual center
since ancient times, and still in parts is "the seat

of wantonness in women."
Words for it in most languages have a secondary sense of "center."

Meaning "center of country" to contemplate (one's) self to
"meditate"—to be.

V.

My editor tells me, this isn't a book about nothing.
You're trying to convince yourself love exists.

VI.

Where she carved an absence has become my omnipresence.
Portal into person. There's no getting in, nor out. I'm trapped
in this whirl of half-birthed things.
I cannot love wholly, only
obsess in
a where
of us.

VII.

Navel-gazer, get out of your own way.

Is it her or me I put my tongue in?

The first dangous thing that lived on Earth.
brontascropina stinger as the size of a lightbulb.
hardshell scorpion
Dragonfly zilla
flesh eating spiders
killar whale
The most Powerful shark in the world
A cenapeed as big as a car
The bigest reptile on earth
skeleton vikings
chasm of Death
The Haunted cruise
Zombie presedents
Evil robot
Jungle of misery
Plates of Whoa
Lava falls
Stegasauras
Evil Tiger
Evil pooh Bear.
Zombie kristerfer robin
Whale
force field
medro
dead
eletric wall

3/8: Bone Letters

(one side of a correspondence)

dear maxilla,

it's your own teeth, not me, who left you an empty mouth. useless. fact: the american revolution was nearly lost because of washington's oral decay; red coats intercepting george's love letters to his dentist would read, "*send more morphine to location X*". british bullets would then travel to X. consider your loss as a gift of infallibility. young men will not die because of your toothaches. i have suckled your gold replacements—your new smiles substantial as honey. however, nothing can replace pulse. part of you now artificial—bites like a machine. george won the war when he gave up his bones. will this be a love letter when i give up you?

dear clavicle,

your name means "little key." did you know? originally a key was a status symbol—necklace advertising the need to defend property. like a crucifix. what do you protect? origin. keys were made not only to fit a lock, but to resemble the doors they opened. names give more names than cows have milk. Sometimes i imagine you turning in me like dynamite in a dolphin's restless eye. dead whale. 3 years have passed yet every day still feels like tuesday. you promised to never mention that other bone to me again.

it's 4 a.m., i don't know but writing this makes the space between us seem taller.

dear humerus,

records show one has one chance in 2500 of breaking you in the course of a year, one chance in 1600 of breaking a femur. but there are many other bones—many other years—many chances of breaking at least once in a lifetime. mostly traffic accidents. some cultures are known for deforming bones deliberately. bind a baby's head. heighten the arch of a foot. this requires breaking. child bones heal faster. it all happens with bleeding. teeth are the exception. teeth crumble. my mom called today. said she has two regrets: not enough family dinners, not enough dental hygiene.

dear coccyx,

how can you call me sacrum? sacred? cross bone? you unfinished tale. tell me, who do you picture when addressing my bones? philosophers? prayer causes fallacious reasoning—a reinforcement of superstitious thinking. touch a loved one who has died and never dream about them (i'll cut off our hands). dream of washing a face and find a necessity for atonement (i'll cleanse us with soil). do these solutions seem reasonable to you? have i finally found liberation from circular? or is this just another fucking prayer?

dear temporal,

a yeti scalp is kept in a glass box at a khumjung monastery, yet given the lack of conclusive evidence, the abominable is regarded as legend. give me a fist full of tic-tac-toe parts and i'll say you have no proof of my red balloons. i let them go once. by accident. our white sheets drenched in flight. you gave me a sponge soaked in light, told me to wash it out.

dear malleus,

so, you've been thinking in millimeters of snot and piss—what does that exact? shit. where i come from—200 pounds is a sin. to be large as weightless sound, we pull nails, hair and skin from our guts. to be beauty in the eyes of nightmares, we flush our flesh away. please, no more talk of loss. my anvil, even for just the length of a song, make that this.

dear tympanic,

i wrote to the whole of you once, but without reply. i have been meticulous. i have gathered the dust of every room you ever occupied. i have cooked your living dead parts into a batter. i have constructed a cake in the shape of a beach house. i lit it on fire. i told you to blow it out. i sang years onto you. all this i for you. i'm begging, try to hear the thing listening.

dear first metatarsal,

the postman misread your address; he added an r and hit a nerve instead of bone. this will happen when numbers get tired. ulna sent the shock to my sister and i, metacarpus, pinky and ring. we have different ideas about your spittle and storms. i'm little and broken, she naked and covered in eczema. we argued for months over the possible conclusions.

dear occipital,

you've stopped speaking in tongues. without facts, you are the ghost in my room. after all this pink, how luxurious fear feels—like a coat made of broken highs. i'm not one to turn a dial for function. i like the surprise of changing pictures.

dear vomer,

i picture you as a series of interlocked secrets. some nights all their hands let loose, i freefall but with debt and furniture.

pre-distal phalanges,

10% of all humans ever born are alive right now. as for your superstitions? a bird in the house is a sign of death. entire cities without 13th floors. if you see almonds in your dreams you have an appointment with sadness. while if you dream of eating ham it means you will soon lose something that means a lot to you.

dear mandible,

at its least, immunity is worth a direct response. recently, i've been wearing another man's weight to forget my own—my failure to eat away my own flesh. communion. you know, sometimes i eat to purge—make a mistake for the satisfaction of taking it back. gagging has more to do with my empty bank account than love. i've been taught god loves those with savings. i would like to be solid as god's love of accounting. i dream of shedding like paper—of giving myself as a substance of matter. to be an offering; but what do bones equal?

dear whateveryouarecallingyourselvesthesedays (maxillae),

been pruning dead roses, burning mulch for light, tossing around an apple. quiet enough to hear fire, i waterlog the future. this is how we land: hip upon rib. it means nothing. but. there could be a solution buried in this overlap, yes? yes is the only answer allowed.

dear lateral cuneiform,

without you, there is no shape. the heart collapses. the nervous system overpopulates itself with strangers. the warmth of rooms escapes me. no marrow, no holding milk, no osteocalcin. no brave leaps into other. without you, there is an innumerable absence. no infinity is worth this.

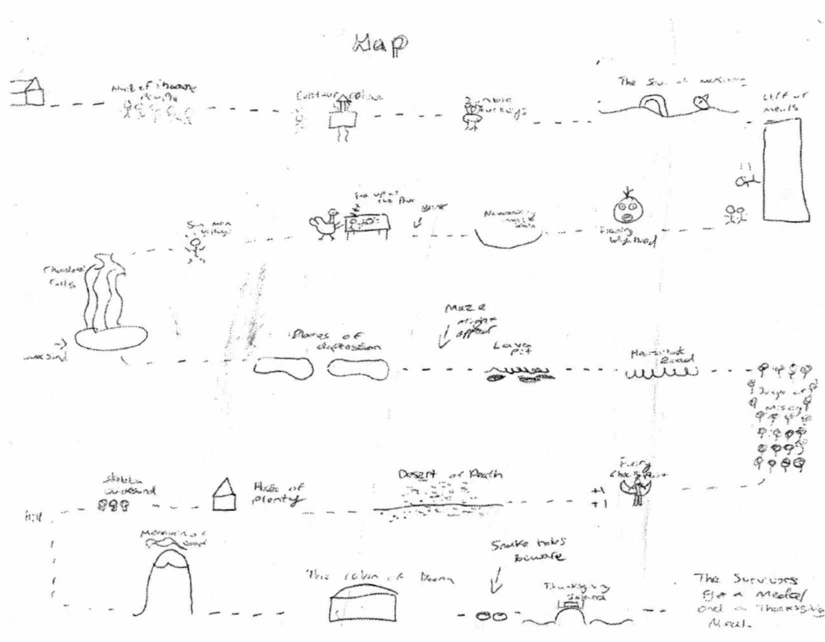

Map
Cliff of
Chocolate
Falls
Maze
might
appear
Lava
pit
Desert of Death
House of
plenty
+1
+1
Snake holes
beware
The Survivors
get a Medal
Meal.

1/2: In Tells

Belly Poem #3:
In the History of Shoes Made from Human Flesh

I.

The dried flesh clicks under my fingernails,
sound of little feet scurrying out from
the severed belly button. A psychological
collapse—
this unexpected drum—
something like the oddity
of holding
one's own
hand.

Is it my hand or taut skin making music?
Are we touch
or touched
when it comes to self-soothing? Skin to skin—

I can't tell me from her—this her that is no
longer hers.
In my hands—does she become mine?

II.

In this:

something like a fairytale—
something like glass—
something like the gouged-out
eyes of stepsisters.

Don't you think?

What became of the heel?
What becomes of the toes?
What do you see in the red

Rorschach test of severed women's parts?

III.

I both recoil and delight at judgment—how it brings
all things closer
and at the same time further from me.

This girl who is not here, yet fully present
in my hands.

Can gossip summon her spirit back to flesh?

IV.

In other news:

Train robber Big Nose George Parrott became a fancy pair of shoes after he died of…

In other words:

A play is written from the perspective of Magda Goebbel's high heel shoes made of…

In other ways:

Hitchcock had his belly button removed for many reasons including a phobia of…

5/8: Course Contents

Introduction[1]

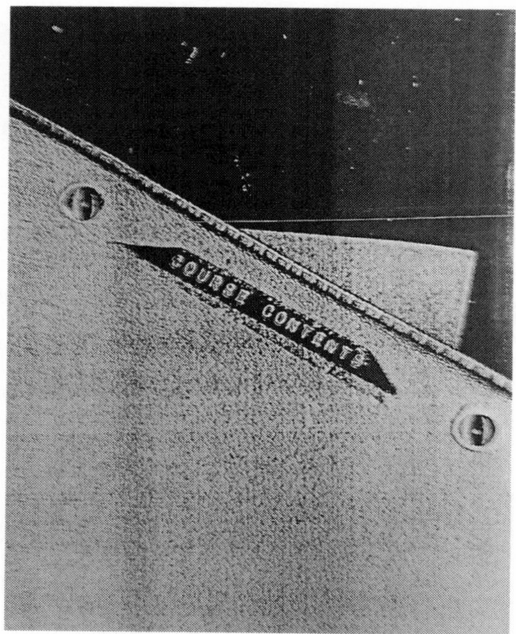

Course Contents is a collage poem made from images and texts taken from a two-volume binder set of a 1960's charm schoolteacher. Her 9-week class was divided into 6 lessons: makeup, wardrobe, figure control, visual poise, personality, and voice. When she set about developing, opening, and graduating her first charm school class, she was diagnosed with cancer. She knew she was sick; she didn't expect to die eight months after her diagnosis. With a husband and seven-year-old son, she left this world with these binders; her final note in the margins of beauty is "who am I."

[1] Here is the game: I dress like a soccer mom / teacher (my most worn costumes). Underneath is something tighter. I take things on and off as a visual strip / on tease, until I feel myself a dominatrix. I pick 6 contestants, I mean students, I mean victims. They must do what I say, until they have something to say about it.

a collage poem /
interactive performance
a poetic "experience"
made from a two vol.
binder set made by a
1960's charm school
teacher
When she set about
developing, opening,
and graduating her
first charm school
class, she was
diagnosed with
Cancer
She knew she was sick;
she didn't know she
would die 8 months after
the diagnoses
With a husband
and seven year old
son, she left this
world with these
final notes written
in the margins
"Who am I?"
TALKING MARIONETTES
THIS IS HAZELLE
with some of her favorite marionettes
Hazelle Hedges Rollins began creating Hazelle's Marionettes 17 years ago and personally designs all characters. With a background of artistic ability and training, coupled with exceptional ingenuity and creative talent, her hobby of making marionettes has grown into an international business.
Who am I?
Am I the kind of person who enjoys
being center of attention? or a follow
quietly attractive.

Table of Contents[2]

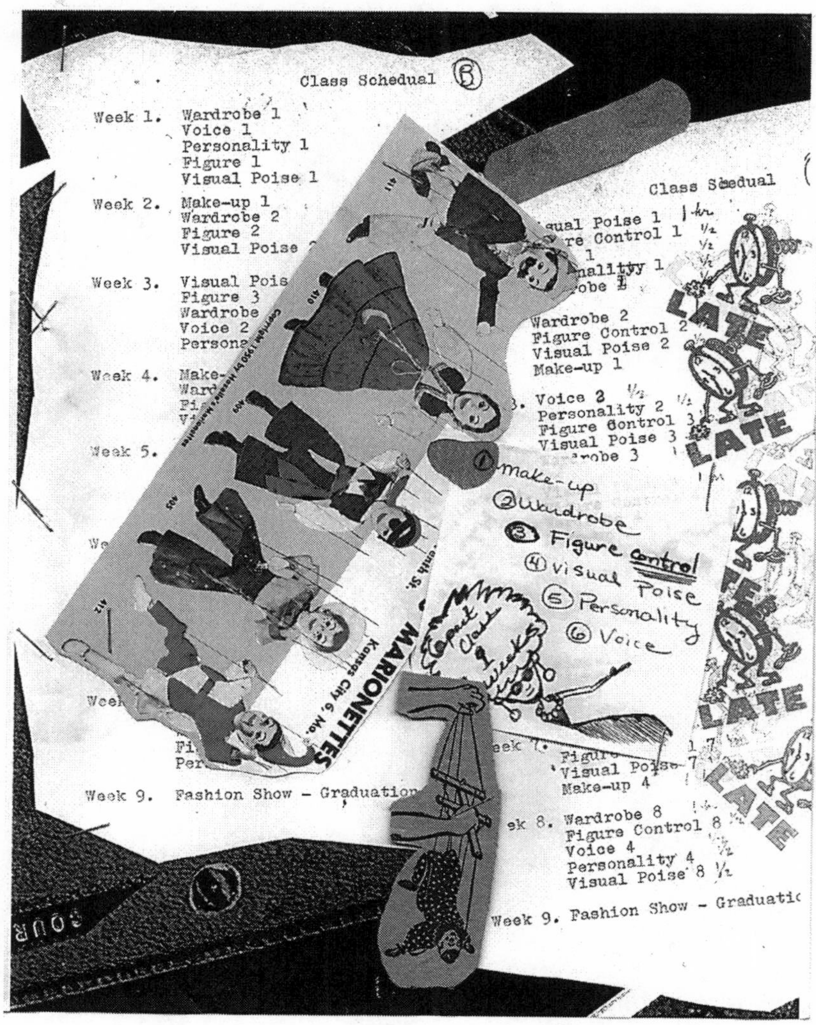

[2] We are all so tired, but don't want to feel dead. We are not dead yet. Repeat it. We are not, we are not, we are NOT DEAD YET.

Lesson One: Make-up[3]

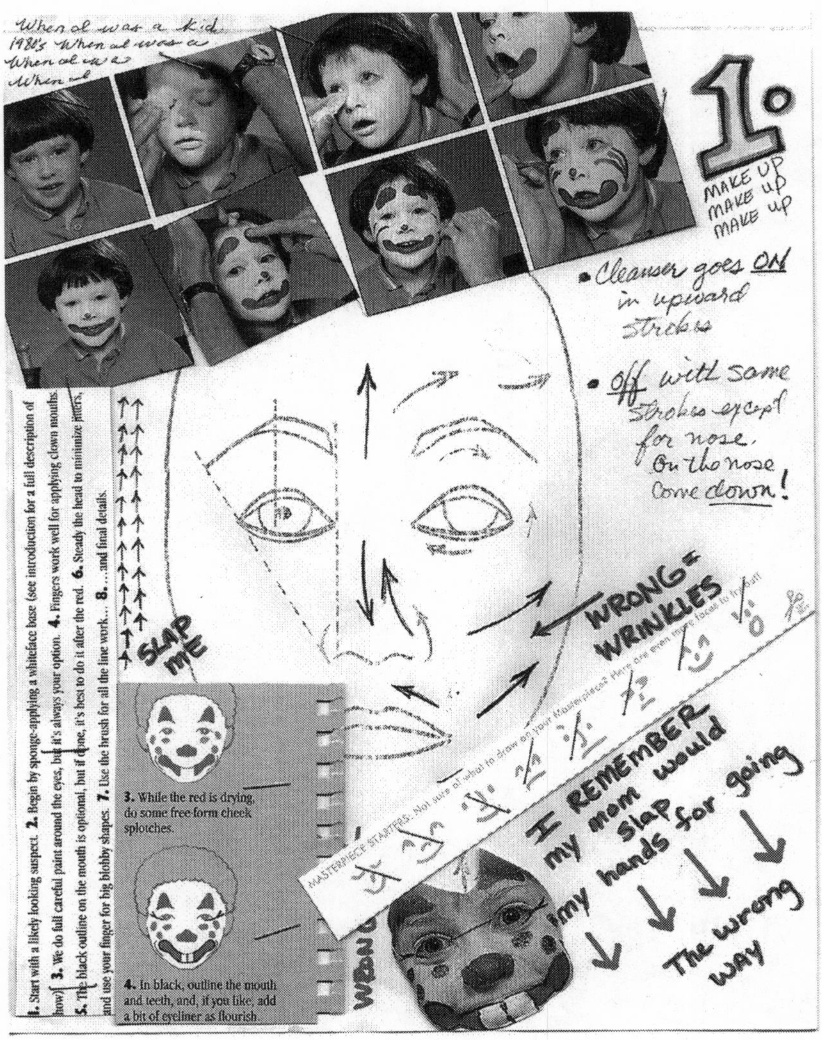

[3] I asked him to paint a picture of his mother using makeup. He realized most makeup is designed to look like blood and bruises. I licked his tears in approval.

Lesson Two: Wardrobe[4]

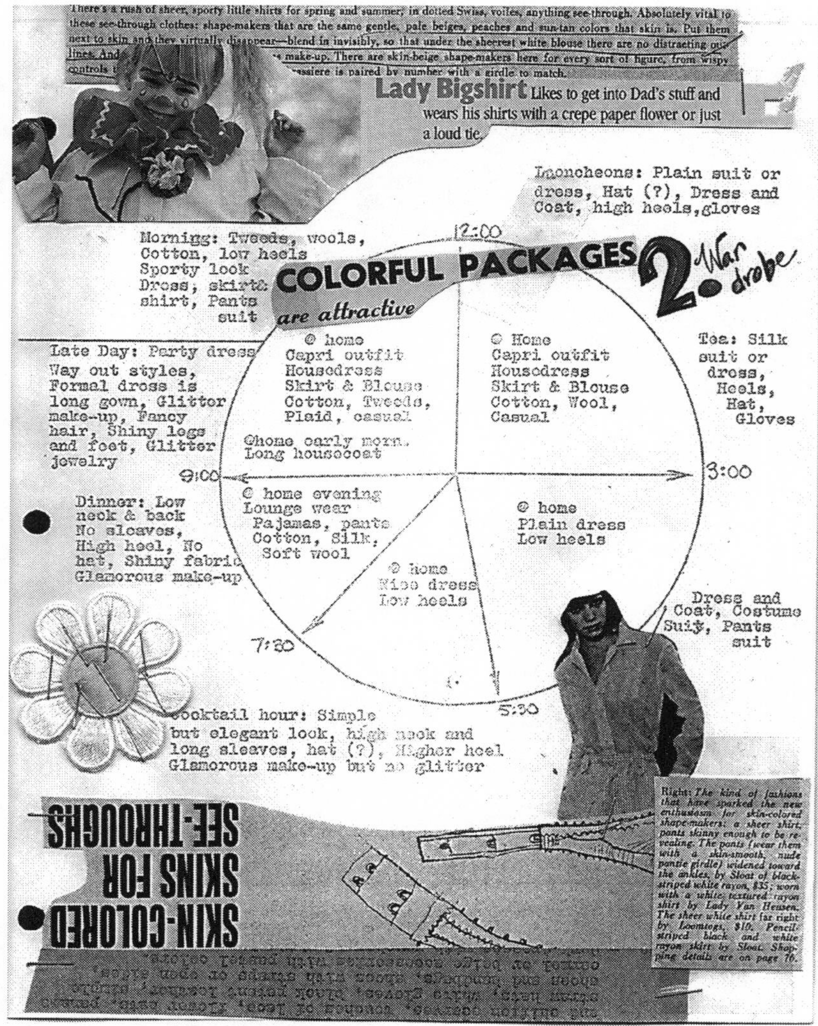

There's a rush of sheer, sporty little shirts for spring and summer, in dotted Swiss, voiles, anything see-through. Absolutely vital to these see-through clothes: shape-makers that are the same gentle, pale beiges, peaches and sun-tan colors that skin is. Put them next to skin and they virtually disappear—blend in invisibly, so that under the sheerest white blouse there are no distracting out
lines. And
make-up. There are skin-beige shape-makers here for every sort of figure, from wispy
controls
assiere is paired by number with a girdle to match.
Lady Bigshirt Likes to get into Dad's stuff and wears his shirts with a crepe paper flower or just a loud tie.
Loncheons: Plain suit or dress, Hat (?), Dress and Coat, high heels, gloves
Mornigg: Tweeds, wools, Cotton, low heels Sporty look Dress, skirt& shirt, Pants suit
12:00
COLORFUL PACKAGES
are attractive
2. War drobe
Late Day: Party dress Way out styles, Formal dress is long gown, Glitter make-up, Fancy hair, Shiny legs and feet, Glitter jewelry
@ home Capri outfit Housedress Skirt & Blouse Cotton, Tweeds, Plaid, casual
@ Home Capri outfit Housedress Skirt & Blouse Cotton, Wool, Casual
Tea: Silk suit or dress, Heels, Hat, Gloves
@home early morn. Long housecoat
9:00
3:00
Dinner: Low neck & back No sleeves, High heel, No hat, Shiny fabric Glamorous make-up
@ home evening Lounge wear Pajamas, pants Cotton, Silk, Soft wool
@ home Plain dress Low heels
@ home Nice dress Low heels
Dress and Coat, Costume Suit, Pants suit
7:30
5:30
Cocktail hour: Simple but elegant look, high neck and long sleeves, hat (?), Higher heel Glamorous make-up but no glitter
SKIN-COLORED SKINS FOR SEE-THROUGHS
Right: The kind of fashions that have sparked the new enthusiasm for skin-colored shape-makers: a sheer shirt, pants skinny enough to be revealing. The pants (wear them with a skin-smooth, nude pantie girdle) widened toward the ankles, by Sloat of black-striped white rayon, $35; worn with a white textured rayon shirt by Lady Van Heusen. The sheer white shirt far right by Loomtogs, $10. Pencil-striped black and white rayon skirt by Sloat. Shopping details are on page 76.

[4] They must put on and take off. Mostly take off. "Please make it stop," he tells me, "I'm exhausted." "Put the fucking dress back on," I tell him, "Now take it off." He fumbles with the bra. "What you don't know says a lot about you," I warn the audience. They laugh. He grows red in the face. It's the best look he's put on all night.

Lesson Three: Figure Control[5]

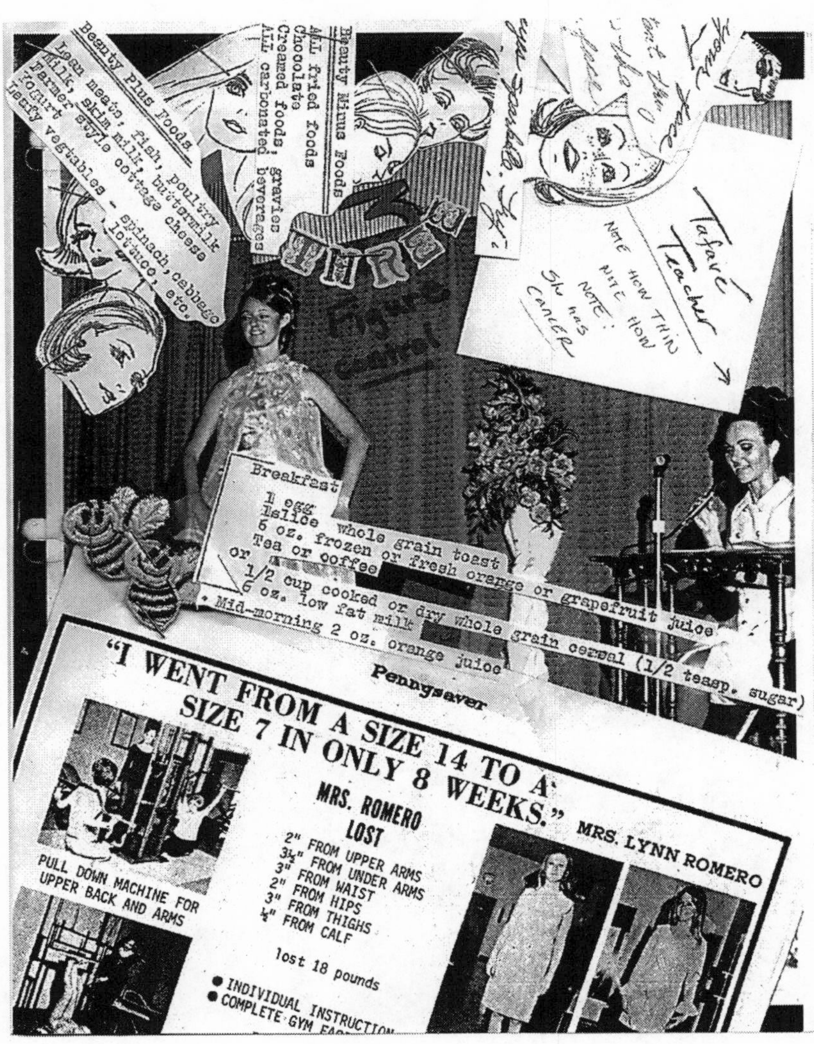

[5] "You can taste, but don't swallow," I tell her. She chews and spits, chews and spits. In front of all these people, chews and spits. "This is the most flavor I've had in three months," she tells me. She smiles, and I make her stick her tongue out until it's dry. It begins to swell. Some might call this punishment, but she keeps smiling.

Lesson Four: Visual Poise[6]

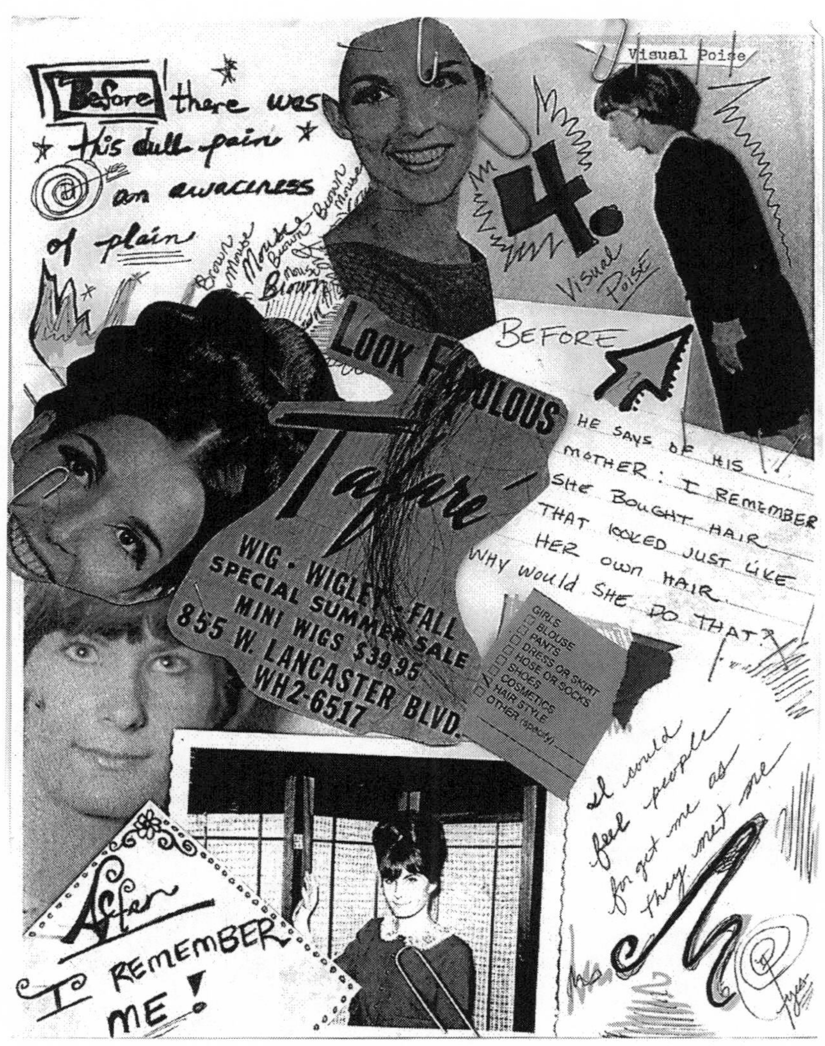

[6] See next page for footnote.

Hairstylist Sam Villa—Premiere Orlando Main Stage

—*The very hairs of your head are all numbered* (Matthew, 10:30)

```
//////////////////////////////////////////////////////////////////////////////
[He lifts a            woman's severed head—her hair            sectioned into
 twelve                 tribes, 4 groups of 3, apostils             and peeks—
 astro      //////////   ////////////////////    ////////////   ////////
 logical    signs—plastic  form, with the wig bundled  into tight spun  buns.]
/////   /////////////   //////////////////////   //////////////   //////
/////   In order to create   /////////////////////   What is important   //////
/////   we have to loosen   /////////////////////   is this: if we do   //////
/////   up our mindsets     ////////////////////    things the same     //////
/////   /////////////       ////////////////////    way we get the   ////////
//////                      /////////////////////   same results.    ////////
///////          ////       ////////////////////    //// ***        //////////
////////////////////        //////   I   //////     //////////////
////We are relying on ///   ////// want //////    ////////////////////
our pattern and disconnection   //// to walk you /////   //////////////////
//to make things happen.//   // through a hair //   ////////////////
  ///////////////////////   ///   cut   //////   ////////////////
   /////////////////////     ///////////////     //////////////
       /////////////////       ////////////      //////////////Disconnection
          //////////////         ///////        is seamless now, it is not as
            ////////////           ////         raw
               ////                    as it was in past; in the past,
                    /////                  if you said
               /////                  disconnection, the clients would
                        ///                freak out.
                    ///               Now you say the word detached
         ///////////////              suggesting more movement, more
         /////////////////                texture.
   Simply turn your chair, cut        ///////////////////////////////////
          the V from the inside.        //////////////////////////
          See the crown pop—             ////////////////////////
               it is detached.           //////////////////
/////////////////////////////              //////////////
    //////////////////////       //        /////////
         /////////////////       So        //////
/////////////////////////        why       //////////
////////////////////////      triangles:     //////////////
  /////////////////////       think inside    ////////////////
      ///////////////          /// out. ///    /////////////////////
Our inspiration comes ///     // Triangles //    //////////////////////
from the past, but it is ///  work as protectors.  /////////////////////////
how it moves forward ///    People can become    ///////////////////////////
that makes it work. /////   very weak in their   //////////////////
/////////////////////       /// temple areas. ///   //////////////////////
I believe in double—be      lieve in double identity   —I believe in double identity.
Let's get rid of the word   versatility, and tell our clients   your haircut has double ident-
```

Lesson Five-A: Personality[7]

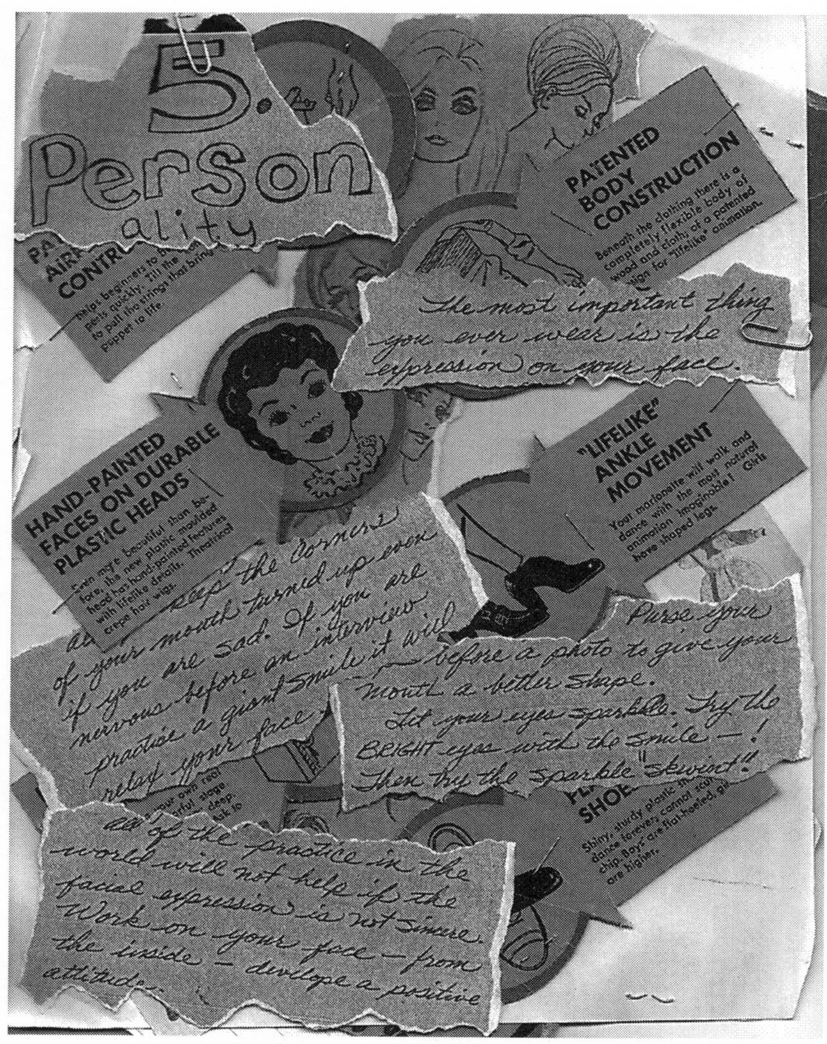

[7]There is nothing so likeable as a mirror. No amount of sadness should ruin your face. Think what you want, but make your face say yes— no matter—nothing is so loveable as nothing. Does it matter if you exist? So long as you seem like what is wanted, that wanted will always be loved. Be a guarantee to have guarantees.

Lesson Five-B: Personality[8]

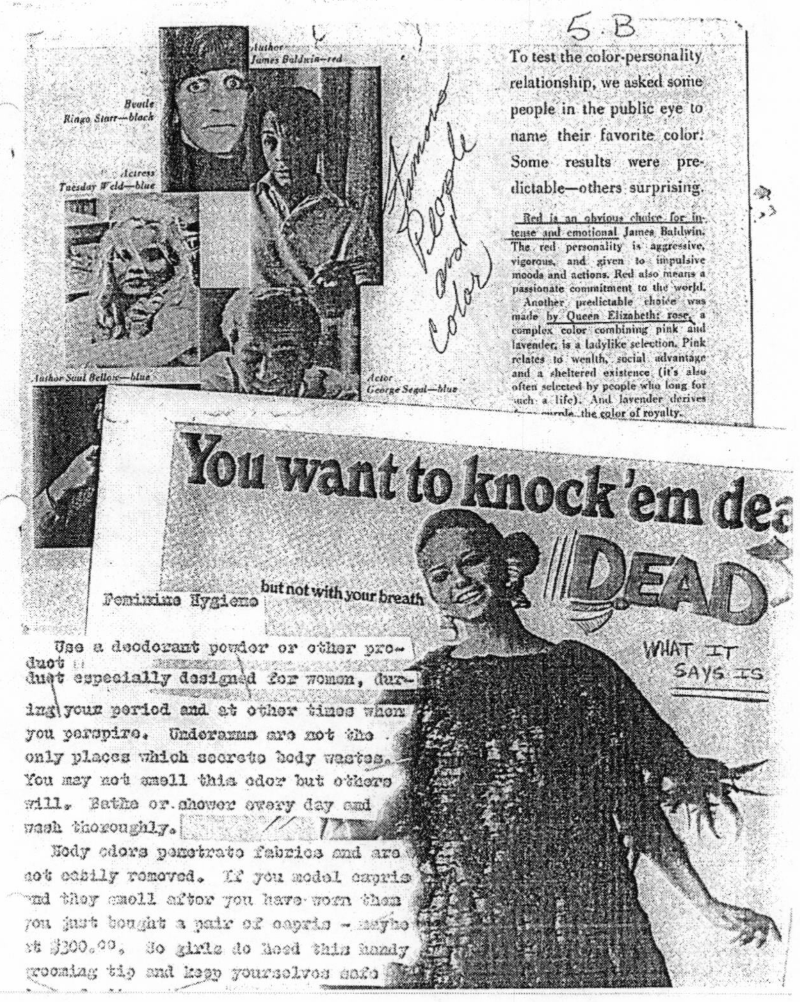

To test the color-personality relationship, we asked some people in the public eye to name their favorite color. Some results were predictable—others surprising.

Red is an obvious choice for intense and emotional James Baldwin. The red personality is aggressive, vigorous, and given to impulsive moods and actions. Red also means a passionate commitment to the world.

Another predictable choice was made by Queen Elizabeth: rose, a complex color combining pink and lavender, is a ladylike selection. Pink relates to wealth, social advantage and a sheltered existence (it's also often selected by people who long for such a life). And lavender derives ... purple, the color of royalty.

Feminine Hygiene

Use a deodorant powder or other product
duct especially designed for women, during your period and at other times when you perspire. Underarms are not the only places which secrete body wastes. You may not smell this odor but others will. Bathe or shower every day and wash thoroughly.

Body odors penetrate fabrics and are not easily removed. If you model capris and they smell after you have worn them you just bought a pair of capris - maybe at $300.00. So girls do heed this handy grooming tip and keep yourselves safe

[8] "Your pussy is not easily removed. Model capris and they smell after you have worn them—that is a $300 loss. They smell like you—they smell like your period and perspiration. You are period and perspiration. You are sex and shame. You are shame. Hide that shit. Hide it. Hide you. I want to see all of that deodorant stick smeared into your crotch. Smear that crotch. Smear it." I say and they do.

Lesson 6: Voice[9]

6. VOICE

Voice and Speech

Telephone Voice

1. with a smile Hello?
for an office "Name of Co. May I help you? or "Good Morning — name of Co.?" Particular dept "Engineering, Miss Smith" or "May I help you?" or "Good morning, Engineering"
2. Softly — do not yell into telephone
3. Enunciate every word.
4. Always ask "May I tell him/her who is calling?" Never say "Who's this?"
5. Say "I'm Sorry he is in Conference may I take a message?" "May I have him call you?"
6. "Thank you for calling" "Goodbye" never say "Yeh" and hang up
7. Don't dally!

[9] What sexual innuendos did you use today to have your basic needs met?

Before and After[10]

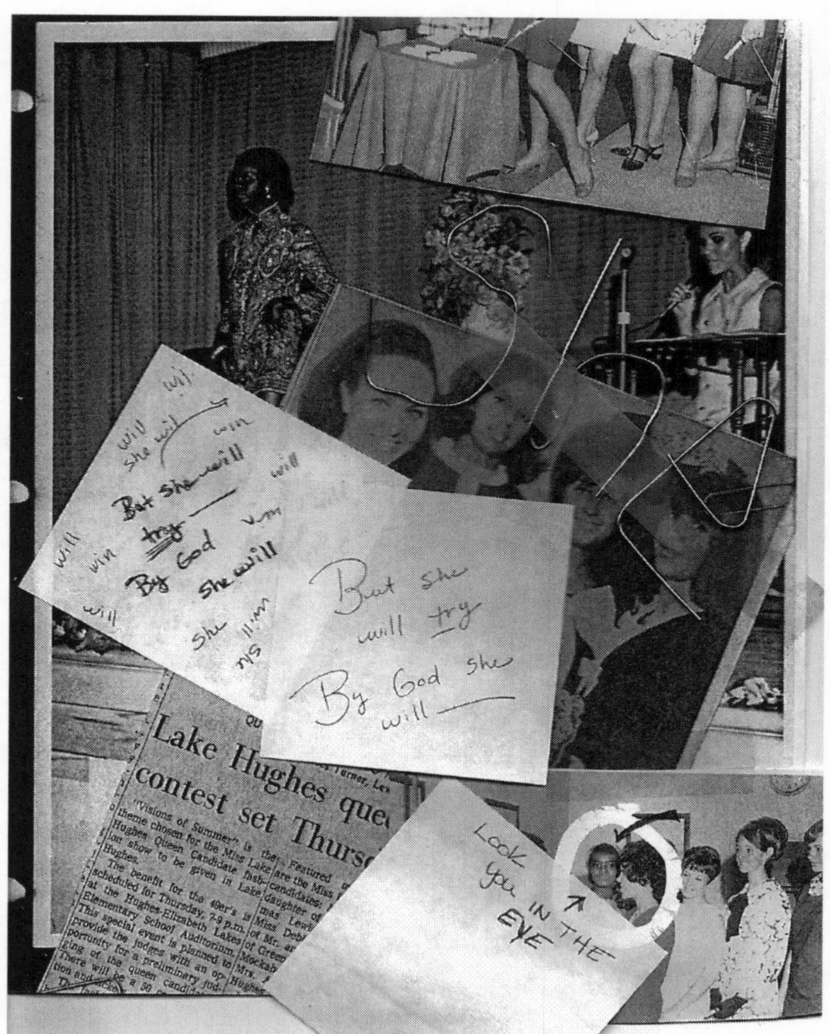

[10] In case you didn't know, "Visions of Summer" is code for unmarried after 30. It's a pageant. Only one can be Queen but winning won't guarantee a husband. Husband (n) "to dwell." You too can be a house, just make a list of who lives inside you—you haunted house—you open door—you a slowly closing uterus, you casket.

Before and After[11]

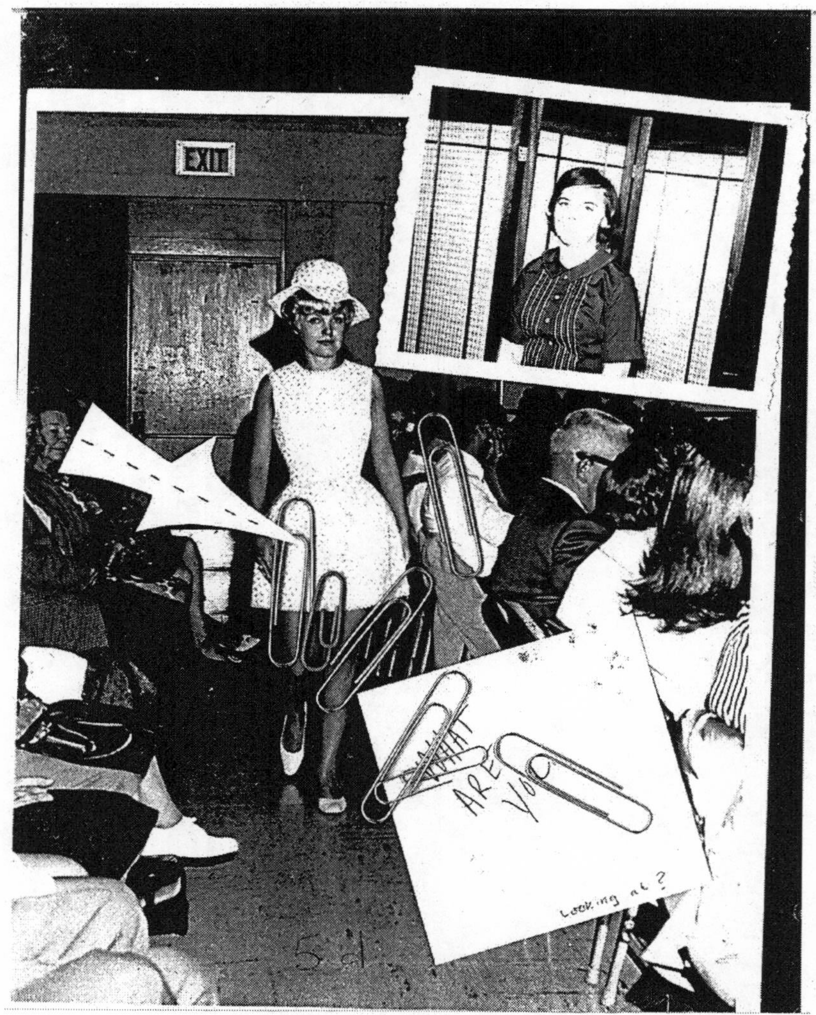

[11] It's not all bad—being born one person to become another. And another. And another. Remove the *who* and so many *whats* become possible.

Before and After[12]

[12] I want the *who* of my (great)(grand)mother, but so much *what* comes between us. How are we to measure gains and losses. This is not a lesson in feminine insecurity. It is a lesson on how I will never really know my (great)(grand)mother, but I have all the instructions to become her.

The Last Letter[13]

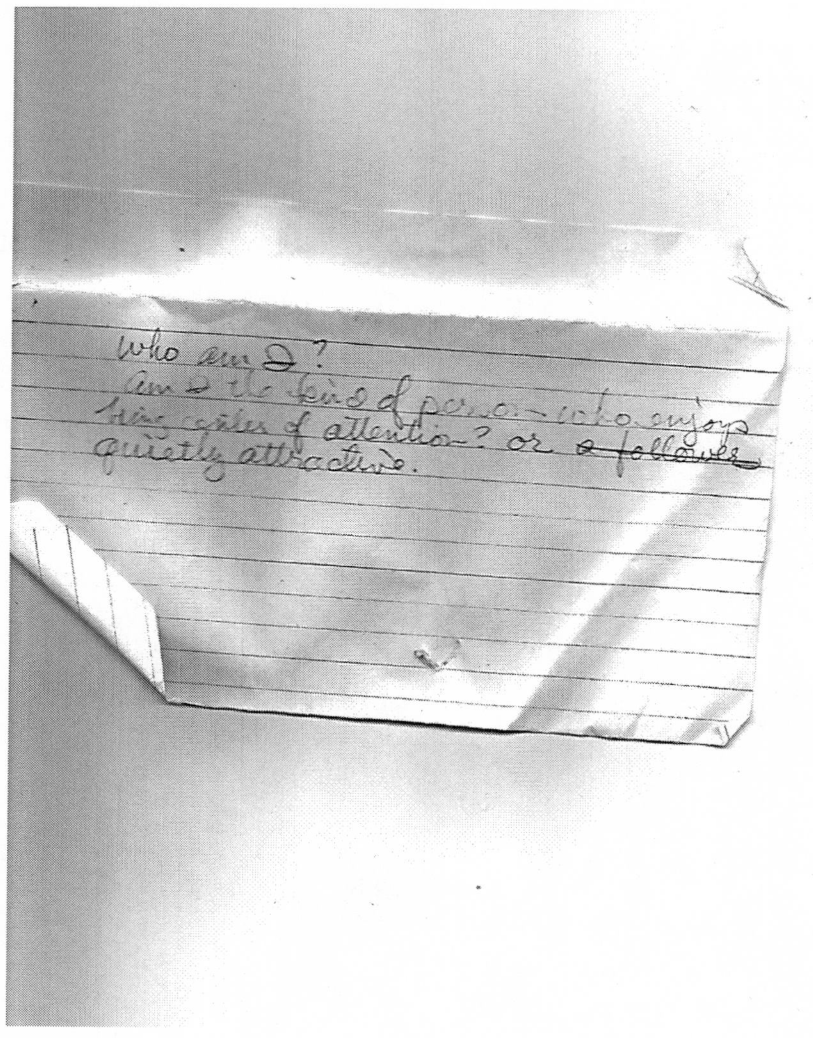
Who am I?
Am I the kind of person who enjoys
being center of attention? or ~~a follower~~
quietly attractive.

[13] Last letter: Who did she think would read it? Was she thinking of you? Do you think the dead are waiting for you? Do you? Do you pass for female? Do we pass? Does the ghost come off in the wash? Are your eyes bleeding black? Want to borrow? my mascara? What part of her is now you?

3/4: In Pieces

Belly Poem #4:
When the Scar Erases the Erasure

I.

Other is just another name for ______________.

A. teacher
B. mother
C. friend
D. lover
E. sister
F. daughter
G. taxpayer
H. dog parent
I. stain remover
J. pacifist
K. killer
L. adoption
M. author
N. hero
O. villain
P. victim
Q. woman
R. believer
S. water
T. drought
U. problem
V. solution
W. you
X. me
Y. belly button
Z. failure (all of the above)

II.

I tell people about the belly button. I tell people I'll never write about the belly button. I say, it's too personal. I say, it's not my story. I say a great deal of things for attention.

My son says to leave his stories alone. He is not casual—his life is not my next poem.

My best friend became my enemy today. He asks, *Why should I have to be the villain and the victim?* So, I can be the hero is the answer and we know it. Heroes are the asshole

of the world. This asshole wants to save a belly button. This asshole wants to save the girl. This asshole is the missing piece of an otherwise finished puzzle. Shit is the world being

taken in and returned to the dirt it came from. What of the world isn't in us? Yesterday

I wrote my name on the bathroom stall with my own piece of god. With my ring finger I spelled *A S S H O L E.* The smell was something like hell. Something about it delightful—

simply because it was. My friend / enemy tells me anything I write will be forgotten in less

than two decades. What I think but don't say is, *I don't give a fuck*. He says, get on my level. He says brick and mortar. He says, my name is on buildings. I start writing about

belly buttons. I start writing about a girl I never knew. I lie and lie and lie until lying

seems all I ever do. Even though I can give proof of the severed skin, can give shitsfor having written, can show you everyone I ever hurt trying to love them. When I tell my cousin, the lead engineer for collision avoidance software, about the bellybutton, about the girl, she looks puzzled. *Wouldn't the scar be much larger than the belly button—*

what is removal if what is left is far larger? I've given you the three people I loved most

in my life and have lost in degrees. Reader—the scar is always larger than the hole.

III.

I have said the words, sorry
I have said the words, love

until I emptied them of meaning.

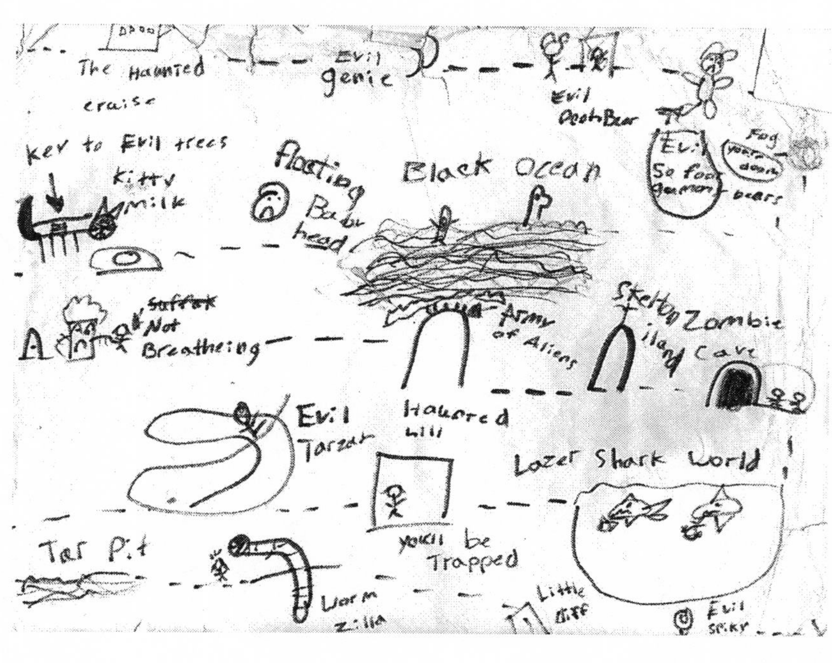
The Haunted craise
Evil genie
Evil DeathBear
Fog
Evil
bears
Kev to Evil trees
Kitty milk
floating
Baby head
Black Ocean
Not Breatheing
Army of Aliens
Zombie
Cave
Evil Tarzan
Lazer Shark World
Tar Pit
you'll be Trapped
Worm zilla
Little Biff
Evil Spiky

1: The Map Game

Without Sky

Their game is this: they draw
monsters resembling a world
built by the generations before
them. When I buy them capes,
they roll their eyes with disgust:
Superheroes are so passé, they say.

Where do kids learn to say *passé* —
how do they know they've come
from zero—O, as in
Out of date, as in
Obsolete?

They say, *if we were to fight for a world
unworthy of saving—we'd fight against
the Old—we'd work our way Out from
the fear you've invented.* They say, *we
can't fly in your broken sky.*

So the Game Begins

—maps made with stolen
pens. From bags and drawers,
permanence
taken. Paths ink
past totems.
Summer nights
stack.
Light
lingers
past beds. Sun on edge.
We lose
a day—searching for
consolations, suns are star
shining
upon the insurmountable.
We draw
the world towards us with lines
fine as kite strings—our paper
lives flying—
out of our hands.
Here is the story of my son
and how he imagined
his way out
from under
his
mOther.

The Map Game Rule Book

1. Set up the board.

To set up **The Map Game** board, unfold and place it somewhere in the real world where everyone can reach it. Inside every fear

is a world. Do not mistake one room for all rooms. Arrival is only the lungful of air before departure. Only by passing through each

knotted threshold can you access realms within your self(s). Like most things, before being lived this will seem horrific, but

remember "horror" is just another word for "ruffling feathers." You're preparing yourself(s) to fly below ground and dig above sky.

2. Shuffle the cards and stack them together in a pile.

Make sure that all cards are facing down, so no player can see what they have chosen for the rest of their lives. Take turns pulling random

motions of confrontation. If this was tarot, we would call it divination,
but since it's just a game, we call it the News. Think about how

the dinosaurs died—now make a wish on a shooting—

3. Place pawns on the start square.

The game comes with character-pawns. Choose an avatar—you have now become a god moving mortal forms around. Already we

are having more fun than before, yes?—all dolls eventually find other dolls and bang their plastic bodies into each other like meteorites—

like the formation of the world—like the making of you—

4. Let the youngest player go first.

Have all players announce their birthdays to determine who
is the youngest; this should make all those suffering from ageism

feel the weight of time holding their heads deeper under water.
Not to worry. Learning to breathe when there is no air is how

we discover new things—like how to grope at the empty spaces
you abhor—go inside zero— remember the word-root for *entry* is
birth.

Context as Threshold

What I see: Four children down a yellow
slide, jump for sky, dive into green
yards, swimming in dirt, leap through pink
hula-hoops.
What they see, can't be seen—story in their bodies,
they hunt gold buried in a giant's rib cage.

Rolling down a house-sized straw, into a juice box.
Drunk-up, they land on the roof of a mouth, lower
themselves down
a damp rope-tongue until, beneath
a heart, they find treasures

Escape, they explain, requires an exit—
we have to be pooped out—
show me what you've found—
I say. They give me a handful of rocks
and call it gold.

The New Winning:
The Map Game Explained by Ages 10, 8, and 6

The Master Mapmaker explains, *it is a game we've designed to win.*

The Mapmaker's Apprentice expounds, *we make maps to fight out from what we fear.*

The Youngest clarifies, *like the Titanic, there should've been a way out for everyone.*

The Master Mapmaker continues, *should have, but wasn't.*

The Mapmaker's Apprentice adds, *yeah, like The Towers—when they fell, no one was ready.*

The Youngest chimes, *we'll be ready.*

Ready for tsunami, hurricane, tornado. They watch them.
On YouTube. And map them.

Global warming is real you know, The Master Mapmaker announces.

More-some will be saved because we played The Map Game, says
The Apprentice.

But not all, The Mapmaker reiterates. *No, not all can be saved.*

The Youngest agrees, reluctantly. He loves The Mapmaker more
than the world.

The Map Game Obstacle One: The First Dangerous Thing That Ever Lived on Earth

The first dangerous thing that ever lived on earth was happy—rolling across mountains with 18 machete legs, waging its hammer-tail while poison drippled liquid rainbows down its abdomen.

It formed iridescent trails as its sneaky fingers tickled itself with sensual antenna. Its eyes dividing and redividing—saw color as viewed from a vibrating bed. It slept on rivers and dreamed of currents—when it

talked in sleep, water kissed its forehead in gratitude for speaking its unspeakable names correctly. When the sun rosed, he bid it good morning. When the moon lilied, he told it goodnight.

All was good until
the First Harmless Thing that ever lived on Earth arrived.

The Map Game Obstacle Two: The First Harmless Thing That Ever Lived on Earth

The word prey and pray fill a mouth with the same shape—mouths opening on the sounds as if to take in food, water, or full kiss. A harmless thing is made for desire, its nature an open valley. Its interior, cupped hands extending with gestures of offering—it says, *take my emptiness, a space for companionship—a hole that is whole self in yearning for acceptance.*

There is nothing more dangerous on Earth.

Parental Reflections on the Known: Stealing the Worlds of Children

I've
begun
to take their
drawings, collect
them in a cage. I like
to hear them sing impossible
tones of endlessness. Time suspended—
brass bars on a chain. I've begun to rub my teeth to
knives, my face crack wide, all of me is going to depths
and edges.

Birds in

me are pacing;
their beaks bleached
to fangs; myth says,
if I bury such teeth
alphabets will sprout.
But I do not long
for letters—
I want

flight. I
ask for wings.
Children draw
two continents
shaped as lungs—
ocean be- tween—
waves jagged
as stairs.

They say,
jump.

Parental Interjection on Freedom: Refrigerator Art #1

The drawing by Age 10 is this:

Her face, a fresh egg, looks out with noticeably different-sized eyes. A dress, made from Magic Markers, has bled a bit in the construction fibers—her body is something of a stain. A heart splits into a gaping hole—this must be her mouth, for this is where
a mouth would go. Her neck is held in a crayoned vice. A giant razor-blade, dangles. Her hair is stacked high as the drawn guillotine—layered yellow circle-curls suggest something electric. A coffin-shaped man stands near, holding a rope. His face is an unlit taper. His smile, a red licorice horseshoe—sweet and lucky. When I ask Age 10 what her picture is about, she says, *It is the beginning of democracy*, slice of cake—enough for everyone.

*****

Parental Response

Dear Age 10,

I was too impressed with how right you sound to say, you're wrong.
When Marie Antoinette told people to eat, she meant she didn't
understand the law of the land— she didn't even have land; she was
land to her husband who was not a man but a metaphor for law.
Few could afford white bread, so bakers gave it freely—metaphor
against metaphor. When asked about freedom, Marie replied
she believed in sweetness—that if bread is free, let it be free.
Only bread is never free. They killed her and so killed a metaphor
and in doing so laws did morph. The guillotine is the perfect
metaphor for pain—death hung from a string—for we can
cut the puppet, but the players always remain. The beginning
of democracy is not in the blade, but in the giving of bread.

Bread, remember, is never free.

The Map Game Obstacle Three: The Children Imagine De-Feeting the Evil Centaur or Confronting Fears of Absolute Freedom

This palace is home with no direction:
the motherless prince puts dishes in
the toilet, food in the bed, doors open
nowhere and windows are without views.
The image of a half-man / half-animal
is something evil, that is, something
half-loved / half-hated. The eldest child
asks if she copulated with a bird, would
she have a winged-child? When asked
where babies come from, she says,
Evaporation. Yes, close enough. From
water lifted by the sun, Centaurus came
from a cloud shaped like god's wife; born
hunched over the arch of betrayal, he slept
with horses because no human would
have him. He was untouchable as our
broken promises. The children fall
to the ground exhausted from running.
They're a heap of many legs and elbows,
a monster attempting to outrun the rain—
the curse of not knowing anything other
than the most wild half of themselves.

The Map Game Obstacle Four: Chicken Noodle Soup Alien or Confronting Fears of the Unknown

There's a chance we all came from discarded bowls of Alien soup.

— The Map Maker, Age 10

The mind tells us that in order to move forward we must control—we must know what is waiting for us out there beyond the asteroid belt. But let's not limit ourselves to noodles. You, little land stars, couldn't have come froma flavor that is described with equal parts relief and disappointment, "tastes

like chicken." No. When the space-portal chucked fatty gristle of broth from its motorhome disposal into the universe, it splattered against the cosmos without a compass. A red dwarf said, "yum, tastes like rainbows" and ateso much it exploded into who is now you—the unknown, where discovery

happens by all means. Extraterrestrials come and go in amazement of how stars cooled into our bodies full of light. They watch us dance and sing, and marvel at how we invent limitations—as if we could limit the expanse of star-stuff. It is said on the dark web, you can tell human fat from animal

in how it congeals into multiple points, unlike the roundness of say a horse or a pig, or a goat, or a hippopotamus, or a bat, or a bird, or a dung beetle. So much of the world can be brought into the self through the mouth. Sing for me now, *Twinkle Twinkle Little Star How I Wonder What You—*

Parental Reflections on the Unknown: Poison Control and the Old Neighborhood

The woman from Poison Control asks, *Do you have the actual?*
I saw the bottle on the counter—saw my son in a thin lake on
the bathroom floor. *I need your help,* I tell her, voice breaking
on itself, *I don't deserve him—*

When Mary Lou from the old neighborhood lost her
son, she drank a bottle of bleach right off the store shelf.
She bolted to the street—steady stream of red pouring
from her, as though a child had the ribbon of her interior
and was running wild with it.

It wasn't Clorox. *It was window cleaner—generic,*
I manage to tell the woman. *Not to worry, she says,*
such things are mild as vinegar. Watch your son

for an hour. I remember as a kid visiting Mary Lou—
her parrot mouth, tongue burned to a cylinder, tooth-
less. She laughed at my staring, told me, *Girl, I wear*
on the outside what love'll someday do to your insides.

Parental Interjection on the Fear of Disappointment: Refrigerator Art #2

The drawing by Age 8 is this:

Thirteen figures—some sticks, others with torsos fleshed to plump raisins, run about the 8 x 11 paper. Some spout interjections like "Run" spelt with a backwards N or "Fu…" "…it." There is, in fact, a bobbed-blonde smiling

from behind a box-shaped counter; she sells apples, bananas, grapes. Just behind her, a volcano is blooming. She looks satisfied, her concession stand the perfect end-of-world business. Who wouldn't want a final taste?

What is this? I ask Age 8. *Pompeii*, she says. In the left-hand corner, two line- thin people sit with a checkerboard between them. I ask her why the couple's not running. She explains, *They're old and are not afraid of dying.*

Above is a mess of brown on top of blue scribbles. *They've been dying for so long,* she says. The sky indicates soon no one will be able to breathe. They understand there's only time for one last…

*****

Parental Response:

Dear Age 8,
I'm too old and not young
enough to play checkers.
Does that make me the con-
cession or blooming volcano?

The Map Game Obstacle Five: The Floating Baby-Head of Doom or Confronting Fears of Consumption

There is a baby without a body—a giant head
floating on a lake of purée. Her mouth always
open, but food flows right through; no place to
put the world, she is pure hunger. The Children

make hand motions; they are swimming on dry land,
while the lake in their heads has them drowning.
The baby wants them, even though no amount of
other can fill her. The Mapmaker warns: *appetite*

will mistake you for applesauce. You must hide,
wait, until she falls into dumpling sleep. Then.
RUN! faster than tear streams—drop your feet
harder than gravity's pull. With the tread of your

shoes, move the world towards the quickened
rotations of happiness. On the other side of this
lake is an invisible orchard. Making it safe to shore,
they can eat themselves full with imagined fruits.

The Map Game Obstacle Six: First, Visit Skeloton Iland

A lump in line implies land. Two
perpendicular marks topped by circles—
a rounded darkness—equals tree. Ten dots
represent sand or footprints in sand.

Here, map-keys are not given, but earned. To know grain
from foot, you must dig in—each bone resembles your name.
The line between land and water is confused by our living forms—
I prick my son's quarry-blisters with a needle,
wrap his soft flesh and send him to master the next mapped
challenge—I limp from imagining his pain.
picture—
an ocean cupped in a skull.
I'm drinking my own brain, he tells you,
and you taste for the first-time sky.

Parental Reflections on the Known: Mothers

After my maternal grandmother died, more doors opened
to small rooms. My mom would disappear into locked
bathrooms with her friend, the woman who fed me tamales.

The woman's daughter and I would play Barbies. Pushing
the micro-pink-plastic lips against Ken's permanent-pantie
crotch, she'd pretend to lick off imagined lines of sugar.

I didn't understand then all the white powder that dusted
everything in our lives. We could write our names on any
flat surface in those days. Inhaling pixie-sticks, my brother

used his bloody noses to wash everything red. Eventually
my father was locked out of rooms too. He'd sit alone
with a half-played game of Hearts. My brother and his

friend would light each other on fire, the fuzz of their
clothes a nova burst before darkness again. Nobody noticed.
When I was 13, and staining all the walls of our house

with practice kisses, my mother took us out for margaritas,
just little ones, to tipsy us towards talking. She wanted to
know if I liked girls. She wanted me to want girls. "Just don't

be half-gay," she would say, "Those people are just greedy."
When her nose bled, she said it was because of her
exceptional sense of smell. She could smell gay people, she

told me. She told me she believed in aliens. Such things
seemed possible with a probed nose like hers. When I told
my mother I liked both men and women, I felt greedy as

invasion. When she said she knew, I understood tamales.
The sky is a slow swirl of stars, constellations leading our
way, none of them asking to be *the answer.* Now I'm a mother.

When given a telescope and microscope, my son prefers
the latter. For hours he sits with his case of glass plates,
smearing his own snot for examination. He keeps a map

of the prehistoric world under his pillow, he dreams of
resurrecting a T-Rexs. When I asked him, "why spittle
and blood before stars," he says,

"there isn't one without the other."

Parental Interjection on Death: Refrigerator Art #3

The drawing by Age 6 is this:
Stacked arches where red paint drips onto
a frantically brushed black sky. *A rainbow
at night*, he tells me. Titled: *The Universe*.

*****

Dear Age 6,

I won't tell you, what can
or cannot exist. Even if
allowing you to keep a U-
niverse requires being a
monster instead of mother.

The Map Game Obstacle Seven: The Bull Vampire / Forbidden Mom Knowledge

The Bull Vampire hasn't a picture; its presence
a sign on the perforated road—
traps of fornication intuited—children
letter their way past adult myths.

What children can't see, comes easiest for moms—
golden heat—Zeus building Europe
in the thicket between their legs—
so many thorns cut before a city rises. Mother's pulse

in the bull's mouth—my life his helmeted idea—
freedom an interpretation—of having no choice.
The back of the beast is a boat—floating beneath
all surface of chance—hear water-voices of children calling,

he cow drowns in its own blood; swim towards a breathable warmth.

The Map Game Obstacle Eight: The Pit

It’s easier to see light indirectly. The path is covered in
berries; by arrival, it seems each step has bled. Red
spreads across the harbor: the day ends with water
holding sky. Washing our feet, the waves appear to be
bleeding. Our distance tastes of brine and berries—
I watch another summer fade, your face, washed in
gold, rotates slowly into night.

A Single Mother's Map

At night,
wonder if the moon
understands solitude,
after years of listening
to the wishes of others
has it formed its own
desires?

In the desert
a hill catches planes before they reach
runways—wings in flames—metal melted
into tears, crows collect flickers for nests,
same as they amass stray balloons, Christ-
mas-tinsel and dropped change.

To find a pocket full of tears, you must
disturb a crow-nest's unbroken weave.
Just this year,
hikers found a boy's arm,
well the bone of it. Lost
in a war not many remain
to speak on, or is that of.

What is the on and of this?
Who held on?
Who was of this?
Bone.

When tested,
birds only take what is needed.
To build a home, they show no
preference for shine—sheen is
what they have to harvest from.

I am warned
what seems big now will seem small.
What seems small will seem large.
Large. And lost.

Sleeping,
my son's face casts back the light
of the moon. This isn't my light—
it is its own brilliance. I watch him
breathing. His breath too large to fit
in my pocket.

We
collect objects because
time doesn't fit in our pockets.

Lover, if I burn you,
don't hate me.
You should have known better
than to treat fire like a fallen piece of the moon.

Other, I offered you
a door that could open anywhere;
you only saw an old brass knob
to set on a shelf.

In my son's pocket
is a bruised dandelion and a fistful of rocks.
"With these diamonds we can see the world,"
my son tells me—*the whole world in my pocket.*
"I can buy us sight," he tells me.
"We'll see," I reply, "we'll see."

My son wakes in the middle of the night—
kicking at a blanket of sweat, he asks—
"Can we live forever? Mommy. I want to live
forever."

How to say yes?—
Teach me how to play your game—the one
with maps and monsters—every location—
limitless. If I can learn this,
I can learn yes.

0: Wholly Love

Belly Poem #5: Emptied

And still I'm sorry.
And still I love you.

About the Author

Nicelle Davis is a California poet, collaborator, and performance artist. Her poetry collections include *The Walled Wife* (Red Hen Press, 2016), *In the Circus of You* (Rose Metal Press, 2015), *Becoming Judas* (Red Hen Press, 2013), and *Circe* (Low Brow Press, 2011). Her poetry film collaborations with Cheryl Gross have been shown across the world. She has taught poetry at Youth for Positive Change, an organization that promotes success for youth in secondary schools, MHA, Volunteers of America in their Homeless Youth Center, Red Hen's WITS program and the AV Migrant Education program. She currently teaches at Knight Prep Middle School.

Acknowledgements

Thank you to the editors who first published these poems, often in earlier forms, in the following venues:

Beloit Poetry Journal, Vol. 61 No. 4
"I Wrote You This Love Letter, You'll Think It's Gross"

Beloit Poetry Journal, Vol. 64 No. 2
"Hairstylist Sam Villa—Premiere Orlando Main Stage,"

Blood Lotus
"Coltrane and Cuba"

Blue Earth Review
"Place—a Pastoral of Amplified Flesh," "First, Visit Skeloton Iland," and "Stealing the Words of Children,"

A Dozen Nothing
"Without Sky," "The Map Game Rule Book," "The New Winning: the Map Game Explained by Ages 10, 8, and 6," "The Map Game Obstacle One: The First Dangerous Thing That Ever Lived on Earth," "The Map Game Obstacle Two: The First Harmless Thing That Ever Lived on Earth," "The Map Game Obstacle Three: The Children Imagine Defeeting the Evil Centaur or Confronting Fears of Absolute Freedom," "The Map Game Obstacle Five: The Floating Baby-Head of Doom or Confronting Fears of Consumption," and "A Single Mother's Map."

Matter Press
"dear maxilla," "dear clavicle," "dear humerus"

Mom Egg Review Vol. 16 –Play & Work Issue
"Refrigerator Art I, II, and III"

Moulin Review,
"Poison Control and the Old Neighborhood"

[PANK]
"Course Contents"

Santa Fe Literary Review
"She Tells You"

Special Thanks

This collection is a long time in the making. These poems span over a decade of writing, and more importantly, they measure an accumulation of friends, family, and poets who have helped me believe in love (poetry).

There are more people to thank than poems in this book, but I'm grateful for the chance to name some of them.

I need to thank Curtis Thornhill, so much of my life is defined by my relationship with you. You have always been my compass, no matter how difficult the journey.

I need to thank Chris and Stan Ulvin, who have loved me despite me.

Those we need to thank are often thanked least and last; please forgive me. Curtis and Chris, you are my foundation; I am so grateful.

I need to thank my Mom and Dad, who taught me to put love first.

Thank you to Eric Morago, who believed in me / believed in this book. Thank you to LeAnne Hunt who copy-edited the dyslexic-mess.

Thank you to Ronald Koertge for being Ronald Koertge.

Thank you to Pavlina Jenson, Anthony Sannazzaro, and the AV kids who inspire me.

Thank you to those who read and edited my work: Peter Schwartz, Carmen Fought, Farnaz Fatemi, Jessica Koong, Seth Hagen, Terry Spohn, Michael Mark, Harry Griswold, Patti Scruggs, P.K. Terri Niccum, Kristen Baum, Shelly Holder, Kathleen Goldman, Elaine Mintzer, Rosie Freed, Aruni Wijesinghe, Robin Axworthy, Nancy Beagle, Alison Turner, Jeremy Ra, Bill Ratner, Hanna Pachman, Curt Hanson, Anne Yale, Andrea Thamm, Annette Schiebout, Missy May, and Adam Smith.

Thank you to those I cannot name but think of daily. This book is as much about failure as it is love.

Thank you to David St. John who gave generously of his time to organize my thoughts.
Thank you to Suzzanne Lummis who made me feel like I could turn a line.

Thank you to JJ and Mike, who are my present tense.

Also Available from Moon Tide Press

Paradise Anonymous, Oriana Ivy (2023)
Now You Are a Missing Person, Susan Hayden (2023)
Maze Mouth, Brian Sonia-Wallace (2023)
Tangled by Blood, Rebecca Evans (2023)
Another Way of Loving Death, Jeremy Ra (2023)
Kissing the Wound, J.D. Isip (2023)
Feed It to the River, Terhi K. Cherry (2022)
Beat Not Beat: An Anthology of California Poets Screwing on the Beat and Post-Beat Tradition (2022)
When There Are Nine: Poems Celebrating the Life an Achievements of Ruth Bader Ginsburg (2022)
The Knife Thrower's Daughter, Terri Niccum (2022)
2 Revere Place, Aruni Wijesinghe (2022)
Here Go the Knives, Kelsey Bryan-Zwick (2022)
Trumpets in the Sky, Jerry Garcia (2022)
Threnody, Donna Hilbert (2022)
A Burning Lake of Paper Suns, Ellen Webre (2021)
Instructions for an Animal Body, Kelly Gray (2021)
*Head *V* Heart: New & Selected Poems*, Rob Sturma (2021)
Sh!t Men Say to Me: A Poetry Anthology in Response to Toxic Masculinity (2021)
Flower Grand First, Gustavo Hernandez (2021)
Everything is Radiant Between the Hates, Rich Ferguson (2020)
When the Pain Starts: Poetry as Sequential Art, Alan Passman (2020)
This Place Could Be Haunted If I Didn't Believe in Love, Lincoln McElwee (2020)
Impossible Thirst, Kathryn de Lancellotti (2020)
Lullabies for End Times, Jennifer Bradpiece (2020)
Crabgrass World, Robin Axworthy (2020)
Contortionist Tongue, Dania Ayah Alkhouli (2020)
The only thing that makes sense is to grow, Scott Ferry (2020)
Dead Letter Box, Terri Niccum (2019)
Tea and Subtitles: Selected Poems 1999-2019, Michael Miller (2019)
At the Table of the Unknown, Alexandra Umlas (2019)
The Book of Rabbits, Vince Trimboli (2019)
Everything I Write Is a Love Song to the World, David McIntire (2019)

Letters to the Leader, HanaLena Fennel (2019)
Darwin's Garden, Lee Rossi (2019)
Dark Ink: A Poetry Anthology Inspired by Horror (2018)
Drop and Dazzle, Peggy Dobreer (2018)
Junkie Wife, Alexis Rhone Fancher (2018)
The Moon, My Lover, My Mother, & the Dog, Daniel McGinn (2018)
Lullaby of Teeth: An Anthology of Southern California Poetry (2017)
Angels in Seven, Michael Miller (2016)
A Likely Story, Robbi Nester (2014)
Embers on the Stairs, Ruth Bavetta (2014)
The Green of Sunset, John Brantingham (2013)
The Savagery of Bone, Timothy Matthew Perez (2013)
The Silence of Doorways, Sharon Venezio (2013)
Cosmos: An Anthology of Southern California Poetry (2012)
Straws and Shadows, Irena Praitis (2012)
In the Lake of Your Bones, Peggy Dobreer (2012)
I Was Building Up to Something, Susan Davis (2011)
Hopeless Cases, Michael Kramer (2011)
One World, Gail Newman (2011)
What We Ache For, Eric Morago (2010)
Now and Then, Lee Mallory (2009)
Pop Art: An Anthology of Southern California Poetry (2009)
In the Heaven of Never Before, Carine Topal (2008)
A Wild Region, Kate Buckley (2008)
Carving in Bone: An Anthology of Orange County Poetry (2007)
Kindness from a Dark God, Ben Trigg (2007)
A Thin Strand of Lights, Ricki Mandeville (2006)
Sleepyhead Assassins, Mindy Nettifee (2006)
Tide Pools: An Anthology of Orange County Poetry (2006)
Lost American Nights: Lyrics & Poems, Michael Ubaldini (2006)

Patrons

Moon Tide Press would like to thank the following people for their support in helping publish the finest poetry from the Southern California region. To sign up as a patron, visit www.moontidepress.com or send an email to publisher@moontidepress.com.

Anonymous
Robin Axworthy
Conner Brenner
Nicole Connolly
Bill Cushing
Susan Davis
Kristen Baum DeBeasi
Peggy Dobreer
Kate Gale
Dennis Gowans
Alexis Rhone Fancher
HanaLena Fennel
Half Off Books & Brad T. Cox
Donna Hilbert
Jim & Vicky Hoggatt
Michael Kramer
Ron Koertge & Bianca Richards
Gary Jacobelly
Ray & Christi Lacoste
Jeffery Lewis
Zachary & Tammy Locklin
Lincoln McElwee
David McIntire
José Enrique Medina
Michael Miller & Rachanee Srisavasdi
Michelle & Robert Miller
Ronny & Richard Morago
Terri Niccum
Andrew November
Jeremy Ra
Luke & Mia Salazar
Jennifer Smith
Roger Sponder
Andrew Turner
Rex Wilder
Mariano Zaro
Wes Bryan Zwick

Made in the USA
Columbia, SC
03 September 2023